Resolving Conflicts at School

Jill Andersen

Rosen REAL READERS

Rosen Classroom™
New York

This is our school's art room.

Art is my favorite class.

Yesterday we drew pictures.
We used markers.

There was a conflict between Brian and Lauren.

They are my classmates.

Brian needed to use
the pink marker.
Lauren needed to use
the pink marker, too.

Lauren took the pink marker.

She would not share it with Brian.

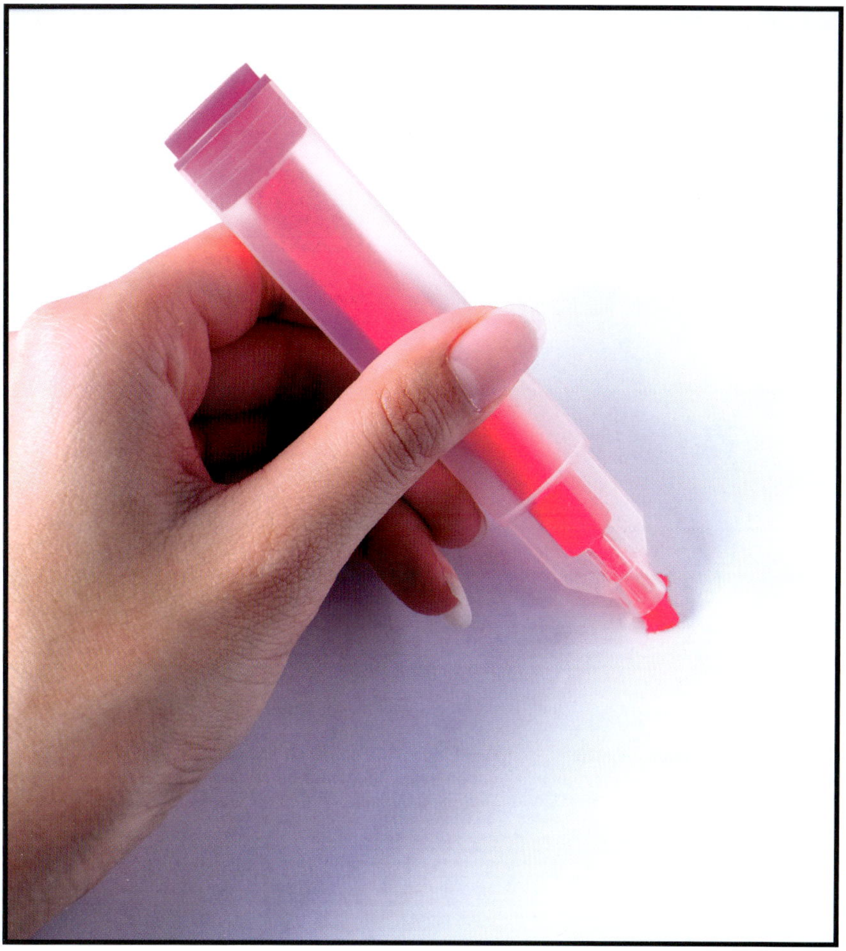

Our teacher had more markers.
She gave a pink marker to Brian.
She resolved the conflict.

Sometimes students
solve conflicts.
Today, Johnny started a conflict.
It happened in the lunchroom.

He cut in front of Jennifer
on the lunch line.
He bought the last apple.
Jennifer was mad at Johnny.

Jennifer told Johnny they should share the apple.

Johnny liked this idea.

He gave the apple to a teacher.

The teacher cut the apple.
Johnny and Jennifer
shared the apple.
The conflict was resolved.

Words to Know

apple

art room

lunchroom

marker